All Things Are Ready

Communion Prayers
For The Church Year
And
Pastoral Occasions

Peter Andrew Smith

CSS Publishing Company, Inc.
Lima, Ohio

ALL THINGS ARE READY

Library of Congress Cataloging-in-Publication Data

Smith, Peter Andrew.
All things are ready : communion prayers for the church year and pastoral occasions / Peter Andrew Smith.
p. cm.
ISBN 0-7880-2487-6 (perfect bound : alk. paper)
1. Lord's Supper—Catholic Church—Prayers and devotions. 2. Church year—Prayers and devotions. 3. Catholic Church—Prayers and devotions. I. Title.

BX 2015.6.S63 2007
264'.13—dc22 2007015440

For more information about CSS Publishing Company resources, visit our website at www.csspub.com or email us at csr@csspub.com or call (800) 241-4056.

Cover design by Barbara Spencer
ISBN-13: 978-0-7880-2487-0
ISBN-10: 0-7880-2487-6

PRINTED IN USA

To all the people
who have walked with me
during my ministry,
and especially
to Meredith,
whose love and support
have allowed me to travel further
than I ever imagined.

Table Of Contents

Foreword

As a newly ordained minister in the United Church of Canada, I found many resources to assist me with prayers and worship service preparation. However I soon discovered that there were few resources with communion prayers and even fewer resources written for seasonal celebrations, especially Christmas Eve and Easter Sunday.

Early on in my ministry, I began to write communion prayers in an effort to make the celebration of the Lord's Supper one which flowed from the seasonal music and which incorporated the themes and scriptures of the lectionary. What follows is a collection of 35 of those prayers and seven different prayers following communion, most of which were written for specific times of the liturgical year. There are also prayers included at the end based upon occasions outside the major liturgical days which may also be appropriate during those times.

Some occasions, like Christmas Eve, have three prayers based upon the same set of readings and a number distinguishes the prayers. Other occasions, like Easter Sunday, draw upon the different lectionary readings and are marked by the corresponding letter of the lectionary year.

These prayers have all been used by me in the congregational celebrations of the Lord's Supper at Trinity United Church in Parrsboro, Grace United Church in Port Greville, and at Quispamsis United Church in Quispamsis. They were originally printed as part of the Sunday liturgy and intended for congregational involvement (bold face sections) but they certainly can be spoken solely by the celebrant. When being tested in different congregations and across denominations during the preparations of this book, the prayers were sometimes modified to reflect the variety of traditions and practices around the table.

Thanks to Reverend Mike Jones, Reverend Greta Smith, Reverend Alastair Anderson, and Reverend Meredith Marple for all their feedback and suggestions.

May God's blessing rest upon you as you come before the table and worship as bread is broken and wine is poured.

— Peter Andrew Smith

Advent, Christmas, And Epiphany

Advent

This prayer is a general prayer for Advent focusing on light and the presence of God with us. The prayers for Epiphany and Transfiguration also use light imagery and could be used during Advent.

The Lord be with you.
And also with you.
Lift up your hearts.
We lift them up to the Lord.
Let us thanks to the Lord our God.
It is right to give God thanks and praise.

Eternal God, we praise and thank you for the hope and peace of this season. For when there is no way your light shines in the darkness. In our lives and in our world you keep us from ruin and despair by your love and mercy.

We thank you for the friends we have known, for the families we have been a part of, and for the strangers who have shown us your will and your way.

Holy God, we praise and thank you for the joy and love of this season. For when we are surrounded by violence and strife you remind us of a better way. In our lives and in our world you call us to be agents of compassion and examples of grace.

We thank you for the times we feel your grace rest upon us, for the words which stir our souls, and for the actions which lift our spirits.

Loving God, we come to this table as the people of Jesus Christ. For you have called us to be the church, to offer you our praise, to receive your blessings, and to go out into the world in your name.

You have charged us with the task of bringing the gospel of Jesus Christ to the world. You call us to holiness and peace in order to send us back into the world to share the words and actions of love.

We gather around your table to taste again the goodness of your promises and the truth of your way. We have come to be renewed and refreshed at your table, to share in your blessings so we might be your blessing to the world.

For on the night before Jesus went to the cross, he broke bread with his disciples. He also took the cup and offered it with his friends. And as he shared it with those around the table, Jesus told them:

"This is my body which is broken for you. Do this in remembrance of me. This is my blood which is poured out for you. Do this, as often as you drink it, in remembrance of me."

We come to break bread and drink wine with the risen Christ. We come to remember and to rejoice in his life, death, and resurrection. We come to recommit ourselves as his disciples.

Send, we pray, your Holy Spirit upon these gifts of bread and cup. Let us eat this bread and taste the bread of life. Let us drink from this cup and taste the cup of salvation. Let us receive the gifts you have provided, for we ask this in Jesus' name.

Amen.

Christmas Eve (1)

Since the Christmas readings are the same for all lectionary years, these communion prayers may be used in any year.

The Lord be with you.
And also with you.
Lift up your hearts.
We lift them up to the Lord.
Let us give thanks to the Lord our God.
It is good to give God thanks and praise.

We do thank you and praise you, almighty God, for you have richly blessed our world through the wonder of Christmas. This is a holy time, a time for miracles, for in this season we celebrate your great gift to us of Jesus Christ.

Down through the ages, your servants walked among the people and proclaimed your love and care. Prophets who called for repentance and right living. Saints who delivered your word. Messengers who told of the coming Messiah.

Holy God, the whole earth needs to hear your word. The message of hope, salvation, and peace needs to be shared with our troubled world. Fill us with your Spirit that we might go from this place and tell of your forgiveness, mercy, and the new life brought by the babe born in a stable.

For on that night, shepherds in the field were keeping watch over their flocks. They saw the splendor of your heavenly host and heard the announcement that Jesus had been born. In wonder, amazement, and hope the shepherds rushed to Bethlehem and saw all that you had done. And they returned home praising you and declaring your goodness.

Loving God, our world needs to know of your goodness. The light and hope of your love need to be shouted from the rooftops and whispered in dark rooms. Fill us with the joy of your Spirit that in wonder and praise we might share your love with all creation.

For on that night, Mary and Joseph saw the fulfillment of prophecy and the unfolding of your promise. They saw the excitement of the shepherds and pondered the meaning of your actions in their hearts. Having experienced your love in action they reacted in faith and hope. They trusted in your way and your promise.

Eternal God, our world needs people of faith. We long to know such people and we strive to be such people. Let your Holy Spirit move through us that we might live faithfully — trusting, believing, and serving in the name of Jesus Christ.

We have walked in darkness but now see a great light, and we know that the darkness can never extinguish the light you send us in Jesus Christ. We have gathered as people who hear the angels proclaiming the birth of the king.

For on the night before Jesus died, he took bread, broke it, and said, "This is my body which is given for you. Each time you do this, remember me." Jesus took the cup and said, "This cup is the new covenant God has made with you in my blood. Each time you do this and drink from this cup, remember me."

We break the bread and we drink the cup. We remember the tiny babe whose birth we celebrate. We remember the man who worked miracles and taught of your love. We remember Jesus who died on the cross and rose from the dead.

We pray on this Christmas Eve that your Holy Spirit might descend upon these gifts of bread and cup. Allow us to feel the wonder, the joy, the excitement, the truth of the first Christmas, the Last Supper, and the first Easter. For we ask in the name of Jesus Christ, who cried from a stable and from a hill.

Amen.

Christmas Eve (2)

The Lord be with you.
And also with you.
Lift up your hearts.
We lift them up to the Lord.
Let us give thanks to the Lord our God.
It is right to give God thanks and praise.

On this holy night, we do praise you. In the midst of the expectation and longing, you have fulfilled your promise to the world by sending the Messiah to be with us.

We who have walked in the darkness have seen a great light. For Jesus, born in this night in Bethlehem, is our hope and salvation.

On this blessed eve, we do praise you. In the midst of our troubled world, you have sent your word of grace and forgiveness.

We who have been lost in sin and death have been reclaimed by your mercy. For Jesus, born this night in a stable, is the Savior, Christ the Lord.

On this night of wonders, we do praise you. In the midst of humble surroundings, you have given us the miracle and surprise of the incarnation.

We who have been silent and unsure have heard the angels sing of your love for us. For Jesus, born this night to Mary, is the source of all our joy.

On this Christmas Eve, we do praise you. In the midst of a humble stable you have come to us as a tiny child. For through Jesus, born this night, we see your love for us made flesh.

We who have searched for meaning and purpose have been shown the way. For you have come among us to open the way, the truth, and the life.

On this holy and blessed night, we give you thanks and praise for Jesus Christ. For through Jesus Christ you have completed the law and shown us the face of salvation.

Through Jesus Christ you invite us to be your people — filled with hope, with peace, with joy, and with love.

For on this special night we remember Jesus Christ; the babe born in the manger; the boy who grew in wisdom and stature and found favor with you.

We remember the man who taught us of your love and worked signs and miracles to show us your kingdom. We remember the Savior who died upon the cross and rose from the grave.

Send your Holy Spirit among us, we pray. That we might join the choirs of angels in proclaiming the salvation of Jesus Christ,

that we might be amazed with the shepherds at your wondrous actions,

that we might offer our gifts to the newborn king along with the wise men,

that we might live as your people this blessed night and all of our days.

Send your Holy Spirit and bless this bread and this cup, so that through them we might experience the mystery and wonder of your grace.

Amen.

Christmas Eve (3)

This prayer makes specific use of the familiar Christmas Eve lesson from Luke 2:1-20 with the congregation answering in the prayer with the familiar verses of scripture.

The Lord be with you.
And also with you.
Lift up your hearts.
We lift them up to the Lord.
Let us give God thanks and praise.
It is right to give God thanks and praise.

This holy eve our voices combine with the choirs of angels and all of creation in praise and celebration. For the Lord of lords and the King of kings has come down from heaven and the goodness of God has spread out to the ends of the earth.

"Glory to God in the highest and on earth, peace, good will to all."

Immanuel, you blessed us at Bethlehem by coming as a tiny babe. In the barren land among humble people you chose to share your life with us. You took flesh so that all the world might know the face of God.

"For unto us is born this day in the city of David a Savior, who is Christ the Lord."

As one of us you matured and grew. From that tiny babe adored by shepherds and travelers from the east, you grew into an adult who proclaimed the way of God. Through your miracles and words, your stories and healing, the world knew the love of God.

"Come, let us see the thing that the Lord has made known to us."

You walked from the stable at Bethlehem to the cross at Calvary. You showed us the way of grace and peace, of mercy and love. With your friends you broke bread and taught them the meaning of sacrificial love.

"This is my body which is broken for you. Each time you do this, remember me."

You also shared the cup. With it you taught them that God had not forgotten the covenant but had instead renewed it in a wondrous and miraculous way. Through your love and grace our lives have been reconnected with each other and with you.

"This cup is the new covenant which God makes with you in my blood. Each time you drink from this cup, remember me."

Send we pray, your Holy Spirit upon these gifts of bread and cup that through them we might celebrate your birth, honor your life, and rejoice at your resurrection. May the bread we eat this night be for us the bread of life through which we remember your sacrifice for us. May the cup we drink from be the cup of salvation through which we recommit ourselves to you this night and always.

Amen.

Epiphany

This prayer is specifically written for Epiphany (January 6) as it makes specific reference to the arrival of the Magi and draws from Matthew 2:1-12.

The Lord be with you.
And also with you.
Lift up your hearts.
We lift them up to the Lord.
Let us give thanks to the Lord our God.
It is right to give God thanks and praise.

God of wonder and light, we do give you thanks and praise. When the people longed for release from sin and despair you responded. When the world was at its darkest you sent your light to dispel the shadows of fear and brighten the colors of life.

"For unto us is born this day in the city of David a Savior, who is Christ the Lord."

God of joy and celebrations, the news of your Savior spread through the songs of angels and the excitement of shepherds. Good news of great joy was spoken in many places. And people came to know of your great light in the form of a baby born at Bethlehem.

"Where is the child who has been born king of the Jews? For we have observed his star and have come to pay him homage."

God of mystery and purpose, you have revealed the meaning and importance of Jesus Christ in many ways. Through signs, words, and actions people have experienced the truth of your love and salvation. You have brightened our world and inspired us to share your light with others.

They saw the child and knelt down and paid him homage. Then they offered him gifts of gold, frankincense, and myrrh.

You offer us the greatest gift, O God, in the person of Jesus Christ. For you did not merely come to be among us. You came to share with us the way of grace and peace, of mercy and love. Among us, you broke bread and taught the meaning of sacrificial love.

"This is my body which is broken for you. Each time you do this, remember me."

With the cup, you taught that the covenant was being renewed in a wondrous and miraculous way. Through your love and grace, our lives have been reconnected with each other and with you.

"This cup is the new covenant which God makes with you in my blood. Each time you drink from this cup, remember me."

We remember, God of grace and glory, the birth of Jesus, his life, death, and resurrection. We come before this table to renew our commitment to you and to experience again the mystery of our faith.

Christ has died, Christ is risen, Christ will come again.

Send, we pray, your Holy Spirit upon these gifts of bread and cup that through them we might know again your light for our lives. Free us from whatever hinders us from serving you and fill us with your love and grace. For we ask this in the name of Jesus our Savior and Lord.

Amen.

Baptism Of Jesus (A)

The next three prayers all focus in on the baptism of Jesus. While they are appropriate for early in January, they can also be used on a day when the sacrament of baptism is bring celebrated.

The Lord be with you.
And also with you.
Lift up your hearts.
We lift them up to the Lord.
Let us give thanks to the Lord our God.
It is good to give God thanks and praise.

God of heaven and earth, we do give you thanks and praise. For in the beginning, your Holy Spirit hovered over creation and all things were brought into being. You fashioned the sun and stars, the oceans and rivers, the deserts and mountains.

You breathed life into the fish of the sea, the birds of the air, and the animals of every land. You created men and women in your image. Then you looked at all of creation and called it good.

God of the law and the prophets, we praise you for your mercy. For when we, your beloved creation, turned away from you and fell into sinful ways, you did not abandon us. Instead your Holy Spirit inspired women and men of faith to call us back to you.

In the fullness of time you came as Jesus of Nazareth to complete the law and the prophets. When Jesus came to be baptized, the Holy Spirit descended upon him as a sign of the new creation you offer. Through Jesus Christ, you have opened for us the gates of salvation and the way of eternal life.

God of our salvation, we thank you for Jesus Christ our Savior. For through Jesus we are saved and called to be the church. We thank you also for the Holy Spirit who witnesses to the truth of your promises made to us in Christ. For the Holy Spirit descends and blesses your people with gifts and power.

We thank and praise you for Jesus Christ who has shown us the way and for the Holy Spirit who inspires us and challenges us in our faith. For we can change our lives and our world through faith and service.

You have given us the Holy Spirit to be an active witness and visible presence in the world. Through the Holy Spirit, the waters of baptism become a visible sign of your grace and forgiveness.

Through the Holy Spirit, the bread and wine become for us signs of the death and resurrection of Jesus Christ and these common items become for us a way to experience your divine love and grace.

Send your Holy Spirit among us, we pray, to bless this gift of bread and cup. Allow the bread to be for us the broken body of Christ, a sign of your mercy and forgiveness.

Allow the wine to be for us the blood of Christ, through which you bring about the new covenant binding us to you forever.

Send your Holy Spirit, we pray, that we might rise from this table filled with new strength and hope to boldly live and witness in Jesus' name.

Amen.

Baptism Of Jesus (B)

The Lord be with you.
And also with you.
Lift up your hearts.
We lift them up to the Lord.
Let us give thanks to the Lord our God.
It is good to give God thanks and praise.

In the beginning, gracious God, out of your will and by your word all things were brought into being. The hills and mountains, the seas and rivers, all creatures large and small are the result of your handiwork. This day we thank and praise you for the beauty of creation and the wonder of nature.

In the beginning, eternal God, you made man and woman and breathed your Spirit into them. Out of love and care you made people to live for you and each other. You gave them all that you had created and offered them the richness of your love. This day we thank and praise you for the gift of life, ours and those around us.

But over time people turned away from you, merciful God. They spurned you and all you had given them. They chose to be selfish and ignored your love and call. Yet you did not abandon them in their foolish choices. This day we give you thanks that you have not forgotten or abandoned us in our sins, but that you continue to help us and guide us.

For you reached out to all humanity, loving God. You sent men and women of faith to call people back to you and to your love. Again and again you offer hope, renewal and new life. For you treasure all of creation and every man and woman. This day we praise you and thank you for your unfailing love and mercy.

In the fullness of time you sent your Son, Jesus, to come and live among us. Born in a humble stable, he grew in wisdom and favor in your sight. Through his baptism by John in the Jordan River, we know of your offer of salvation for the whole world. For there you proclaimed Jesus as your beloved Son and let your Spirit rest upon him. This day we thank and praise you that Jesus Christ brought your love and mercy for all of us to know.

During his time among us, Jesus lived his life and prepared himself for the cross. On the night before he died, he took bread, broke it, and said, "This is my body which is given for you. Each time you do this, remember me."

He also took the cup saying, "This cup is the new covenant God has made with you in my blood. Each time you do this and drink from this cup, remember me."

This day we thank and praise you for the gift of holy communion through which we stand before you and know your goodness.

On this day we come before the table prepared for us. We do so knowing the grace you offer to us through baptism and the strength you give to us in this meal. As we come, we pray that your Holy Spirit might descend upon this table that by the presence of the risen Christ we might be renewed through your love and by your grace.

Amen.

Baptism Of Jesus (C)

The Lord be with you.
And also with you.
Lift up your hearts.
We lift them up to the Lord.
Let us give thanks to the Lord our God.
It is good to give God thanks and praise.

Holy scripture tells us, eternal God, that your Spirit moved in the formless void and creation came into being. Your Spirit moved over the waters and dry land and all of the earth was created.

We give you thanks and praise that you have made this world for us.

Holy scriptures tell us, merciful God, that your Spirit descended like a dove upon Jesus as he knelt in the Jordan River and was baptized by John. Your Spirit moved and all knew that Jesus was your beloved Son.

We give you thanks and praise that you have sent Jesus to be our Savior.

Holy scriptures tell us, loving God, that your Spirit came as tongues of fire upon the disciples as they waited in the upper room on the day of Pentecost. Your Spirit moved, and men and women of faith were filled with vision and hope, purpose and excitement.

We give you thanks and praise that you fill us with spiritual gifts and abilities.

We have come on this day to remember and celebrate what we find in the pages of holy scripture. We celebrate your word through which we find meaning and purpose. You have given us the Bible as a light for our lives.

We give you thanks and praise for the record of faith and your holy laws and commandments.

We have come to this church to remember and celebrate baptism. For through baptism you give to us a sign of your forgiveness and the new life we find through Jesus Christ. In the waters of baptism we become one with Christ, sharing his death and resurrection.

We give you thanks and praise for your love and mercy which we receive through baptism.

We have come to this table to remember and celebrate the Last Supper. For on the night before Jesus died, he broke bread and shared the cup with his followers. Jesus said to them "Do this in remembrance of me. This is the new covenant which God makes with you through my blood."

We give you thanks and praise for the bread of life and the cup of salvation.

Send, we pray, your Holy Spirit, upon this bread and cup that as we share this meal we might grow closer to you and to each other. Allow us to know the presence and the power of Jesus Christ our Lord, in whose name we gather, and in whose name we pray.

Amen.

Transfiguration (1)

These prayers all focus in on the Transfiguration texts but can also be used during the season of Epiphany itself.

The Lord be with you.
And also with you.
Lift up your hearts.
We lift them up to the Lord.
Let us give thanks to the Lord our God.
It is good to give God thanks and praise.

We thank you, O God, for your gift of light in creation. We thank you for the spectacular sunsets which hint at your glory and the gentle rays of dawn which chase away the darkness. We thank you for the mysterious moonlight and the soft light of the stars and heavens above us.

We thank you, O God, for your gift of light within us. We thank you for the light of human life, and for the illumination of hearts and lives through your Spirit. We thank you for the witness of the women and men, your saints of every age, who have brightened our world through their faith.

And above all God, we thank you and praise you for the light of Jesus. For through Jesus you have shown us your glory and love; through him we have a luminous example and a shining way to follow. Through Jesus, we who have walked in darkness have seen a great light.

This morning we come before you in praise and thanksgiving. We have seen the wonders of your light with our own eyes. We have experienced your light reaching out to cut through the darkness. We have felt the warmth of your light touching our souls.

In the brightness of your love, we come to this table. We take the bread and cup as signs of your light and life.

For with his disciples, Jesus took bread, broke it, and said, "This is my body which is given for you. Each time you do this, remember me."

He also took the cup saying, "This cup is the new covenant God has made with you in my blood. Each time you do this and drink from this cup, remember me."

We pray, O God, that your Holy Spirit might shine forth on us this day. Through this table let us know the truth of your glory, let us see the wonders of your love, and let us be strengthened to serve as your people.

For we ask in the name of your Son, Jesus Christ, the one who revealed your glory on the mountain and followed your will upon the cross, in the name of Jesus, whose death and resurrection have brought life and light eternal to the world.

Amen.

Transfiguration (2)

The Lord be with you.
And also with you.
Lift up your hearts.
We lift them up to the Lord.
Let us give thanks to the Lord our God.
It is right to give God thanks and praise.

All glory is yours, God most holy. In all of the universe, none is more worthy of praise and glory, service and devotion.

No one is perfect but God in heaven.

Through your love and by your grace, you have invited us to be your people. The pages of the Bible witness to your invitation to share in your glory and in the unfolding of your kingdom.

Your word is like a lamp to our feet.

Yet we are uncertain and hesitant even as you raise up leaders and teachers to show us your way. We are reluctant to believe in your unfailing love and bountiful grace.

The Word became flesh and lived among us and we have seen his glory.

For you came among us as Jesus of Nazareth, speaking words of hope, showing signs of grace, and inviting everyone to see your love.

From his fullness we have all received grace upon grace.

In Jesus Christ we have seen your way, heard your truth, and been offered renewed life in this world and eternal life in the world to come. For in Christ, all your glory came to rest as the disciples saw upon the mountain when he stood as one greater than the greatest prophet and the giver of the law.

Through Christ all things are possible.

As your people, called by Christ, we have gathered at this table to remember and to celebrate your gifts to us. Through this bread we remember that Christ gave up everything for our sakes and died broken on a cross.

By his wounds we are healed.

We also drink from the cup remembering that through it you made the new covenant with us. Through Christ and by Christ we are brought back to you and know of your mercy and pardon for our sins.

In all these things we are more than conquerors through him who loves us.

As we eat and drink, we pray that your Holy Spirit might move among us that we might know again your great love for us. Fill us with the hope of the resurrection and the assurance of the cross that we might go from this place telling of your goodness and sharing in your grace. For we ask this of you, God most holy, in the name of Jesus Christ and by the power of the Holy Spirit, one God forever and ever.

Amen.

Lent
And
Easter

Lent

The references in this prayer to the covenant makes it especially applicable to Lectionary Cycle B, however the general theme of the prayer is applicable for any year in Lent.

The Lord be with you.
And also with you.
Lift up your hearts.
We lift them up to the Lord.
Let us give thanks to the Lord our God.
It is good to give God thanks and praise.

We thank and praise you, God of love, for you desire us to know you. You made a solemn covenant binding yourself to the descendants of Abraham and Sarah. You renewed that vow through the commandments and law.

You give us the law and commandments so we might live as your people.

We thank and praise you, God of grace, for in every generation you are faithful. When your people were enslaved in Egypt, you sent your prophet Moses to lead them to freedom. When the disciples were uncertain and afraid, you sent your Holy Spirit to inspire and direct them.

You break into our lives with light and hope when our world is at its darkest.

We do thank and praise you, God of mercy, for you do not forsake those who turn away from you. Instead you call through prophets for the people to turn back and know your love. Instead you send men and women of faith to lead and teach your people.

You call us to follow and know the truth of your word instead of abandoning us to sinful ways.

As a church of Jesus Christ, we have come to this table to remember and celebrate your eternal love, mercy, and grace. For this is the table where Jesus took bread, broke it, and gave it to his followers saying, "This is my body which is given for you. Each time you do this, remember me."

With this bread, we remember the body of Jesus broken on the cross.

With this bread, we celebrate the resurrection of Jesus.

The broken bread is your promise to take our brokenness and make it whole by your love and through your grace.

We also come before this table to share from the cup. For this is where Jesus took the cup saying, "This is the new covenant God has made with you in my blood. Each time you do this and drink from this cup, remember me."

With this cup, we remember the blood of Jesus shed on the cross.

With this cup, we celebrate the salvation and eternal life we know through Christ.

This cup is your covenant with us. The promise of forgiveness, mercy, and eternal life, not because of our worthiness but because of your love.

Send, we pray, your Holy Spirit upon these gifts of bread and cup that for us they may become the body and blood of Jesus Christ. Allow us to experience again the truth of your word and the power of your covenant sealed by the cross and resurrection. For we ask this in name of Jesus Christ our Lord.

Amen.

Maundy Thursday

This prayer is applicable for Maundy Thursday as it recounts the Exodus and ties it into the Last Supper.

The Lord be with you.
And also with you.
Lift up your hearts.
We lift them up to the Lord.
Let us give thanks to the Lord our God.
It is right to give God thanks and praise.

It is right to praise you, gracious God, for you are a God of hope. When the people of Israel were trapped in slavery, you acted through your servants Moses and Miriam to bring hope. Through them you spoke of salvation and your promise to be their God.

You continue to bring hope into our world. For amidst the despair of the world, you have offered us the way of Jesus Christ. Through Jesus, we have been given the message of hope and life eternal.

It is right to praise you, eternal God, for you are a God of salvation. When the people of Israel were trapped between the Red Sea and Pharaoh's army, you parted the waters and allowed them to escape to freedom. When all seems at its darkest, you act to make salvation sure and certain.

You continue to ensure salvation in our world. For despite the sinful ways we choose, you show us the way of Jesus Christ. Through Jesus, you answer us with forgiveness and mercy.

It is right to praise you, merciful God, for you are a God of new beginnings. When the people of Israel left their bondage you led them to a new land, a promised land. You showed them a land flowing with milk and honey for them to live in and grow as your people. When you act in the world, you cause new life and new beginnings to take place.

You continue to allow new life in our world. For the destructive ways of our world do not stop you from offering us the way of Jesus Christ. Through Jesus you open up for us a new life in this world and eternal life in the world to come.

It is as your people that we come before this table, loving God. For it is as Christians that we gather to remember the saving actions of Jesus Christ and to celebrate the forgiveness and mercy of your love to all people.

Gathered here this morning we remember that on the night before he died, Jesus took bread, gave thanks for it, and shared it with his followers. We remember that Jesus took the cup, gave thanks for it, and shared it with his friends. We remember and celebrate what you have given and continue to give to us in Jesus Christ.

We pray for your Holy Spirit to descend upon us and upon these gifts of bread and cup. Allow us to see and hear and taste your goodness and mercy. Fill us with strength, wisdom, and renewed vigor to live as your people. This we ask in Jesus' name.

Amen.

Easter Sunday (A)

These three communion prayers are written around the Easter stories for the gospels highlighted in the church year. Any of them would be appropriate for the Easter story from John.

The Lord be with you.
And also with you.
Lift up your hearts.
We lift them up to the Lord.
Let us give thanks to the Lord our God.
It is good to give God thanks and praise.

We praise you, God of mercy, that when the women went to the tomb, they found it empty. When all seemed lost and the disciples had given up hope, you were not finished. When the world was at its darkest and Christ lay in the tomb, you acted to give the world light and hope renewed.

We praise you, merciful God, that you act in times of desperation. When your people suffered under the hand of Pharaoh in Egypt, you sent Moses to free them and take them to the promised land. When they strayed from the law and fell into sin, you sent prophets and leaders to guide them. When the world had lost its way, you came as Jesus to offer life and hope.

We rejoice, God of life, that your angels told the women that Christ had been raised from the grave. That joyful news changed the world on Easter morning. Darkness gave way to light, despair to hope, and sorrow to joy. For the impossible was now possible; the unthinkable was now reality.

We rejoice, living God, that you continue to change the world through Christ. We celebrate that the gospel is as rich and meaningful this day as it was when first proclaimed. With disciples throughout the ages, we shout, "Christ is risen from the grave, Hallelujah!"

In celebration of the resurrection, we come to this table. We take the bread and cup as signs of hope and life. For with his disciples, Jesus took bread, broke it, and said, "This is my body which is given for you. Each time you do this, remember me."

We break the bread and we remember.

Jesus took the cup saying, "This cup is the new covenant God has made with you in my blood. Each time you do this and drink from this cup, remember me."

We drink from this cup and we remember.

We remember and rejoice in the salvation you have given us through Jesus Christ. We remember and rejoice that you have triumphed over death and sin.

We remember and rejoice with all the peoples of the world as we proclaim that "Christ has died, Christ is risen, Christ will come again!"

Send your Holy Spirit upon us, we pray, that as we eat this bread and drink from this cup we might know again the living Christ among us. Fill us with the joy and enthusiasm of Easter that we might respond with our lives and we might continue to transform the world in Jesus' way.

Amen.

Easter Sunday (B)

This prayer makes reference to the stories highlighted in the Old Testament and gospel through the Lenten season in Cycle B.

The Lord be with you.
And also with you.
Lift up your hearts.
We lift them up to the Lord.
Let us give thanks to the Lord our God.
It is good to give God thanks and praise.

It is right and good to praise you God. Throughout history you have made covenants with men and women of faith. You have made your solemn promises to them, and the blessings of faith have been theirs.

In the days of Noah, you made the rainbow as a sign of your promise to never abandon us to our sins.

In the time of Abraham and Sarah, you gave a child as a sign that you provide a bountiful future for all people of faith.

In the time of Moses, you gave the Ten Commandments so that we would always know your will for our lives.

In the time of Jeremiah, you promised that one day your law would be written in our hearts.

We give you thanks and praise, O God, that you completed your promises through Jesus of Nazareth. For through Jesus Christ you offer us yourself. Through his body and blood, you have taken upon yourself our sins and transgressions. Through Jesus' death upon the cross, you have sealed this covenant and our salvation.

We give you thanks for all of your promises which touch upon our lives and offer us hope and faith. You have made us inheritors of all the promises you made to our ancestors. You have called to each of us to be your people and to share in the bounty of your love and grace.

On this Easter morning, we give you thanks that the women coming to the tomb found it empty. We give you thanks that through Jesus you have opened for us the way to eternal life.

As we come before this table, we remember the promises you make to us through the law and the prophets, and we remember the new covenant you make to us through Jesus Christ.

We remember and rejoice in the salvation you have given us through Jesus Christ. We remember and rejoice that you have triumphed over death and sin. We remember and rejoice with all peoples of the world as we proclaim that "Christ has died, Christ is risen, Christ will come again!"

Send your Holy Spirit upon us, we pray, that as we take this bread and drink from this cup we might know again the living Christ among us. Fill us with the joy and enthusiasm of Easter that we might respond with our lives, so that as your holy people and your holy church we might transform our world in the name of Jesus Christ.

Amen.

Easter Sunday (C)

The Lord be with you.
And also with you.
Lift up your hearts.
We lift them up to the Lord.
Let us give thanks to the Lord our God.
It is good to give God thanks and praise.

God of all creation, on this Easter morning we humbly stand before the cross. For on the cross Jesus was crucified not for any sin of his own but for the sins of the world. Jesus suffered and died to free us from death and suffering. The Son of God went to the cross to bring us light eternal and life everlasting.

In faith we proclaim, "Christ has died!"

Almighty God, this Easter morning we joyfully gather with the disciples around the empty tomb. The words of the angels spread through the community of believers that what Jesus foretold had come true. We have heard and believe that Jesus has been raised from the dead.

In faith we proclaim, "Christ is risen!"

God of grace, this Easter morning we look out into our world with renewed hope. For the Christ who suffered on the cross and rose from the grave has gone on before us. The power of sin and death has been shattered forever. We move into the world with new enthusiasm to teach and witness to Jesus Christ.

In faith we proclaim, "Christ will come again!"

Gracious Lord, this Easter morning we gather in humility and celebration before this table to share in the bread and cup. We break the bread to remember Christ broken for us. We drink this cup to remember the blood of Jesus shed for us.

For in faith we proclaim, "Jesus Christ is Lord."

Living Lord, this Easter morning we rejoice and wonder at the great things you have done and continue to do for us through Jesus Christ. For through your Son we know mercy, grace, and hope.

For in faith we proclaim, "Jesus is the way, the truth, and the life."

Send, we pray, your Holy Spirit upon this bread and cup that we might share in the life, death, and resurrection of Jesus Christ. May this bread be for us the bread of life. May this cup be for us the cup of salvation. Through your grace and mercy, let us be your people through our risen Savior who lives and reigns with you and the Holy Spirit, one God, forever and ever.

Amen.

Pentecost To Christ The King

Pentecost

The Lord be with you.
And also with you.
Lift up your hearts.
We lift them up to the Lord.
Let us give God thanks and praise.
It is right to give God thanks and praise.

We praise you, eternal God, for on the first day of the week you called creation into being. Through the movement of your Spirit, the heavens and earth were formed and shaped. You made each of the plants and animals in our world and gave them life and purpose. You made people to live for you and for each other.

So on this first day of the week, we give you thanks and praise for creation.

We praise you, merciful God, for on the first day of the week you caused the resurrection to take place. Through your will, Jesus who had been crucified and buried was raised from the dead. You shattered the power of death and sin and freed us to know your mercy and grace. In Jesus Christ, you have called us to a new life in this world and in the world to come.

So on this first day of the week, we give you thanks and praise for Jesus Christ our Savior.

We praise you, wondrous God, for on the first day of the week you caused your Spirit to descend as tongues of fire for all to see. Through your gift of the Spirit, wonders took place to show the power and promise of your love. You moved the disciples to go out into the world to tell of salvation and hope. Through the Holy Spirit you have continued to bless Christians and your church.

So on this first day of the week, we give you thanks and praise for your Spirit.

As people of faith, we have come to this table. We take the bread and cup as signs of hope and life. For with his disciples Jesus took bread, broke it, and said, "This is my body which is given for you. Each time you do this, remember me."

We remember Christ's body broken for the forgiveness of sins.

He also took the cup saying, "This cup is the new covenant God has made with you in my blood. Each time you do this and drink from this cup, remember me."

We remember Christ's blood shed for the redemption of the world.

Send your Holy Spirit upon us, we pray, that as we take this bread and drink from this cup we might know again the living Christ among us. Fill us with the hope and strength of your Spirit that we might respond with our complete lives. Send your Holy Spirit that as your holy people and your holy church we might transform the world in the name of Jesus Christ our Lord.

Amen.

Worldwide Communion

The Lord be with you.
And also with you.
Lift up your hearts.
We lift them up to the Lord.
Let us give God thanks and praise.
It is good to give God thanks and praise.

You call to us, eternal God. From our homes, our lives, our families, you call us to be your people. You call us to be rich through your grace. You call us to be bold in our witness.

You call us to be living examples of the words of Jesus Christ and to walk together in faith.

You give us food, Lord of all creation. From the earth you call forth plants and animals to feed us. Each day we sustain ourselves on the bounty of your gift.

We hunger for more than food to nourish our bodies.

You give us the bread of life, Jesus Christ. On the cross Jesus was broken so that our sins might be broken by your love. The bread of life is our promise of new life here and eternal life in heaven.

The bread from this table gives us the spiritual strength to face an uncertain world in the certainty of your grace.

You give us drink, Lord of the rivers and vine. On the earth, you give us the waters and fruits of the land to quench our thirst. Each day we sustain ourselves on the bounty of your gift.

We long for more than earthly drink to satisfy our thirst.

You give us the cup of salvation, Jesus Christ. On the cross the blood of Jesus was shed, sealing the new promise made for us.

The cup from his table gives us a physical sign of the bond which exists with you and between each one of us because of your love.

So we come, gracious Lord. As imperfect people, we come to share in the perfection of your kingdom. As unsure people, we come to be a part of the certainty of your purpose for us.

We have come to this table at your invitation, to eat and drink the bounty you have placed before us and to remember what you have done through Jesus Christ.

Send, we pray, your Holy Spirit upon these gifts of bread and cup. Grant us the presence of the living Christ that we might taste again the spiritual food and drink for our lives. For we ask this in the name of Jesus Christ, who lives and reigns with you and the Holy Spirit, one God, forever and ever.

Amen.

Thanksgiving Sunday

This prayer focuses on food and God's gifts to us so while appropriate for Thanksgiving, this might also be used on World Food Day or a Sunday where the story of Jesus feeding the multitude is read.

The Lord be with you.
And also with you.
Lift up your hearts.
We lift them up to the Lord.
Let us give God thanks and praise.
It is right to give God thanks and praise.

God of all creation, we give you thanks and praise for we are blessed in this land to enjoy the riches of the earth. The apples from the trees, the wheat from the fields, and the fish from the streams are all signs of your goodness to us.

We thank you for the natural world, a world filled with all kinds of good food and drink within it.

God of life, you have given us food not only to sustain us but also to enjoy. In this bountiful world you have included a variety of rich flavors to make eating another one of the delights of being alive.

We thank you for the meals which not only nourish our bodies but allow us to enjoy life.

God of community, when we gather to eat, we are aware that sharing a meal is also an opportunity to build families and friendships. At the table, we not only nourish our bodies but we also build stronger ties with each other.

We thank you for the meals we have experienced over the past year, which we remember not for the food but for the company.

As we gather on this Thanksgiving, keep us mindful of the importance of food and water for our sisters and brothers around the world. Help us to always remember those in need and to keep our hands outstretched.

You have blessed us with plenty in this land. Help us to use this bounty to bless the lives of others.

We come before this table and see the gifts of field and vine laid out before us. Yet as we come to this table, we are remembering a hunger which cannot be filled with bread and a thirst that cannot be satisfied with drink.

We cannot live by bread alone. We hunger and thirst for the eternal to be among us.

We come remembering your love and celebrating your gifts to us. We break bread in thankfulness that through Jesus Christ you have offered to us the bread of life. We share the cup in gratitude, knowing that in Jesus Christ you have forged an unbreakable bond with us.

We remember and we rejoice that through Jesus Christ you have done this for us.

Send, we pray, your Holy Spirit that by what we do here this day we might serve with greater joy, witness with greater certainty, and love with a more willing spirit. For we have come to share these gifts, almighty God, through the power of the Holy Spirit and in Jesus' name.

Amen.

Christ The King (A)

These prayers are specifically written for the last Sunday of the church year. The prayers in the final section "Life of Jesus" would also be appropriate for this day.

The Lord be with you.
And also with you.
Lift up your hearts.
We lift them up to the Lord.
Let us give thanks to the Lord our God.
It is right to give God thanks and praise.

Lord of lords, King of kings, we do praise you. We praise you for Jesus the Christ, who died on a cross and who rose from the grave. For through Jesus you reach out to us in love.

In Jesus, you show us your way. A way that all of us can follow so that we might know forgiveness and hope. A way that calls us to salvation. Through Jesus, you reconcile us to you and free us from the bondage of sin.

In Jesus, you show us your truth. Truth that beckons to us in our daily lives. A truth that completes us and inspires us. A truth which allows us to know your thoughts and actions. Through Jesus you have shown us yourself, holy and wise, loving and compassionate.

In Jesus, you show us life, life that is joyful and confident. You show us life that allows us to serve and act as your people, assured of your love and grace. You show us life that is new and fresh. You show us life that continues in the promise of life eternal. Through Jesus, you have offered us a place as your people, both here on earth and beside you in heaven.

We remember that on the night before Jesus went to the cross, he gathered in the upper room with his disciples. He took the bread, gave thanks and broke it, saying "This is my body which is broken for you. Do this in remembrance of me."

As we break the bread, we remember. We remember that Jesus died for our sins. We remember his asking for others to be forgiven even as he suffered. We remember the body of Jesus broken on the cross.

On that same night, Jesus took the cup, gave thanks for it, and passed it to those around the table saying "This cup is the new covenant which God makes in my blood. Do this, as often as you drink it, in remembrance of me."

We remember the new covenant which Jesus made that night. The unbreakable promise of your love has given us the way, the truth, and the life. We remember and we rejoice that on the third day, your love lifted Jesus from the grave, shattering the power of sin and death forever.

We ask, loving God, that your Holy Spirit descend upon these gifts of bread and cup. Grant that the presence of our risen Lord might be seen and felt here, that our faith might be strengthened, and our lives renewed. For we ask, remembering and rejoicing in the power of Jesus Christ our Lord.

Amen.

Christ The King (B)

The Lord be with you.
And also with you.
Lift up your hearts.
We lift them up to the Lord.
Let us give thanks to the Lord our God.
It is right to give God thanks and praise.

We do praise you, for you alone are eternal, almighty, just, and holy. You are the ruler of all nations, the Lord of all creation, and the sovereign of the universe.

You caused all things to come into being and all things exist because of your will. You are the King of kings and the Lord of lords.

We do praise you, for you shared yourself with us in the person of Jesus of Nazareth. Through Jesus you showed us your way, truth, and life.

Through Jesus, you showed us such great love that death for our sakes was not to be avoided. Through Jesus, we know you as the God of love and mercy.

We do praise you, for through the Holy Spirit you have shown us a vision of your heavenly kingdom. You show us the way in which justice and mercy, love and holiness combine to create a better world and make us better people.

You call us from our sin and sorrow to be your people. You offer us redemption and new life. Through the Holy Spirit, we know you are both our judge and our hope.

In faith, we come before this table to remember and join together as your chosen people. We remember that on the night before he died Jesus took bread, gave thanks, and broke it saying,

"This is my body which is broken for you. Do this in remembrance of me."

And Jesus took the cup, passed it to his friends, and said:

"This cup is the new covenant which God makes with you in my blood. Do this, as often as you drink it, in remembrance of me."

As we eat this bread and drink this cup, we remember Jesus asking for others to be forgiven even as he suffered.

We remember the body of Jesus broken on the cross.

We remember the new covenant which Jesus made for us.

We remember and we rejoice that on the third day your love lifted Jesus from the grave, shattering the power of sin and death forever.

We ask now, loving God, that your Holy Spirit descend upon these gifts of bread and cup. Grant that the presence of our risen Lord might be seen and felt here, that our faith might be strengthened. For we ask, remembering and rejoicing in the power of Jesus Christ our Lord and king.

Amen.

Christ The King (C)

The Lord be with you.
And also with you.
Lift up your hearts.
We lift them up to the Lord.
Let us give thanks to the Lord our God.
It is right to give God thanks and praise.

We do give you thanks and praise, eternal God, for your son Jesus Christ,

the baby born in the humble stable,

the child who grew in wisdom and stature,

the Messiah who shared the good news of your love,

the good shepherd who called people to know their God,

the Savior who died upon the cross for our sins,

the Christ who rose from the grave to reign as our Lord forever.

Through Jesus Christ you have opened for us the way to salvation, shown us the truth of your love, and promised us eternal life.

We thank you, gracious God, that you have chosen us to be Christ's people. Through your Son you have made us a holy church — blessed to know the truth of the gospel and commissioned to share that truth with the world.

We thank you, almighty God, that you have sent us out into the world as apostles bearing Christ's message.

Your word proclaimed by the church challenges us to boldly live the justice and mercy of your kingdom.

Your people of faith working through the church move us to share the gospel through word, song, prayer, and action.

Your Holy Spirit moving within the church inspires us to profess the salvation and hope of Jesus Christ.

For as the people of the crucified and risen Christ, we gather in faith before this meal of bread and wine.

In the name of Jesus Christ, who died and was broken on the cross for the redemption of sins, we break this bread and remember his words:

"This is my body broken for you."

In the name of Jesus Christ, who rose from the grave to shatter the powers of sin and death, we drink from this cup and proclaim his words:

"This is the new covenant which God makes in my blood."

We eat the bread of life and drink from the cup of salvation remembering the life of Christ and the mystery of our faith.

"Christ has died, Christ is risen, Christ will come again."

Almighty God, send your Holy Spirit, we pray, upon these gifts of bread and cup, that through them we might see and hear and taste and know again the truth of Jesus Christ our Lord.

Amen.

Pastoral Occasions

Confirmation (1)

The Lord be with you.
And also with you.
Lift up your hearts.
We lift them up to the Lord.
Let us give thanks to the Lord our God.
It is good to give God thanks and praise.

We thank you God that through the ages you have called for women and men of faith to be your people.

You called to Abraham and Sarah to leave their home and found a great nation.

You called to Moses to free your people from slavery and Miriam to speak your word as you led them to the promised land.

You called to Jeremiah, Isaiah, and the other prophets to tell us of your law and condemn our sinful ways.

You called through Jesus for people to follow your way. Peter, James, John, and the other fishermen followed. Matthew, Mark, and others also answered your call.

You called to Mary and Martha, Joanna and Mary Magdalene, and many others to be your disciples and they came with their gifts and talents.

In every age and in every place you have called to men and women to follow your will and bear your truth to the world.

In every age you have shown your goodness and mercy through the women and men you call to be your people.

You continue to call, gracious Lord. In this generation you have called us to be both disciples and apostles. You have called us to be both a beacon to the nations and servants in the world.

Today, as your people, we reaffirm our answer; before your table we dedicate our lives to you.

For it is at this table Jesus took bread, broke it, and gave it to his followers saying,

"This is my body which is given for you. Each time you do this, remember me."

This is where he also took the cup and shared it with his friends saying:

"This cup is the new covenant God has made with you in my blood. Each time you do this and drink from this cup, remember me."

Send, we pray, the Holy Spirit upon this bread and cup, that we might be refreshed and inspired through your gifts of life and salvation, that we might continue to learn as your disciples and continue to proclaim as your apostles, for we ask and answer in Jesus' name.

Amen.

Confirmation (2)

This prayer could also be used for a church anniversary.

The Lord be with you.
And also with you.
Lift up your hearts.
We lift them up to the Lord.
Let us give God our thanks and praise.
It is right to give God thanks and praise.

We give you thanks for the church. Whatever our age, whatever our background, whatever our race, you have invited us to be one in Jesus Christ.

You have called to us to be the body of Christ in the world.

We thank you for the rich history which is ours in this church. We praise you for the foresight and vision that brought together so many diverse peoples to form this church.

We pray that we might continue to carry on our rich spiritual legacy as a faithful voice in this land.

We thank you for this congregation. We thank you for the people who built this church through their labor, their prayers, and their presence.

We give you thanks for all those who have worshiped here, sang here, and helped to build your kingdom through our life together.

We thank you for those who are making their professions of faith this day. As they are confirmed, remind us again that we are all responding to your invitation to be disciples.

Let us be role models for each other and learn from each other as together we live, serve, and love in Jesus' name.

For as followers of Jesus, we remember that on the night before he died on the cross Jesus took bread and broke it saying, "This is my body which is broken for you. Each time you do this, remember me."

We eat the broken bread and we remember.

And Jesus took the cup and passed it to his followers saying, "This cup is the new covenant God makes with you in my blood. Each time you drink from this cup remember me."

We drink from the cup and we remember.

Send, we pray, your Holy Spirit upon this bread and this cup that we might see and taste your goodness and proclaim your gospel to the ends of the earth. For we ask this of you, heavenly Father, in the name of Jesus Christ, through the unity of the Holy Spirit, one God, forever and ever.

Amen.

Reaffirmation Of Faith

The Lord be with you.
And also with you.
Lift up your hearts.
We lift them up to the Lord.
Let us give thanks to the Lord our God.
It is right to give God thanks and praise.

Almighty God, we thank you that you have invited us to be your people. You came among us as Jesus Christ to call us to be disciples and apostles. You continue to send prophets to proclaim your truth and men and women of faith to share our faith journey.

We give you thanks, God of glory, that you have not wavered in your promises. You richly blessed those who came before us. You continue to offer forgiveness and mercy to all who turn to you.

Loving God, we thank you that you intend a holy purpose for us. You have invited us to use our hands to share your gospel and our words to light the darkness. You have made us the means by which you share grace.

We give you thanks, God of mercy, that you have judged us through the cross of Jesus Christ. We thank you for the mercy, forgiveness, and grace which you have lavished upon us through his death and resurrection.

Living God, we thank you for Jesus Christ. Through Jesus you give us the way to live our lives, you grant us new life here and in the world to come, and reveal to us the truth that transcends the world.

Inspire us, God of grace, to live as Christ's people, being bold and certain in our message and actions. Through our words and deeds, make your message of hope and love come alive.

As Christ's people, we remember that on the night that Jesus was crucified he took bread, broke it, and said, "This is my body broken for you, each time you do this think of me."

He also took the cup and shared it with his friends saying, "This cup is the new covenant made in my blood. Each time you drink from this cup, remember me."

We break the bread and share the cup. We remember Jesus' life, death, and resurrection.

We eat the bread and drink from the cup. We recommit ourselves as Christians.

Send, we pray, your Holy Spirit upon these gifts of bread and cup so that through them we might taste again your goodness and know your grace. With the bread of life and the cup of salvation, fill us with your Holy Spirit to live and serve in Christ's name.

We ask this in Christ, for Christ, and through Christ, in the power of the Holy Spirit. Amen.

Stewardship

The Lord be with you.
And also with you.
Lift up your hearts.
We lift them up to the Lord.
Let us give thanks to the Lord our God.
It is right to give God thanks and praise.

We do thank you and praise you, eternal God, for you call us to be your people and to be your church. Throughout the ages you have called women and men to come to you in faith and to live and serve as your own.

You give us your law as a way to live in love with you and each other. You bless us through teachers and prophets who have called us to your way. You show us love through the goodness of those who surround us.

In your holy church, you call us together. Young and old, from city and country, you call out to us. Blessing our gifts and talents, you challenge us to share the gospel with your creation. Living as your church, we serve and witness in your name. But at times we ignore your call and wander from you.

We thank and praise you that even when we turn away from you, you do not turn away from us. You hold us in a love which cannot be broken, a love so strong that you came and showed yourself to us in Jesus, one who was fully like us and fully like you.

In Jesus you walked with us in joy and in sorrow, in temptation and suffering, and with humility and faith.

In Jesus you showed us the way, the truth, and the life.

In Jesus Christ you showed us such great love that death itself was overcome upon the cross.

We remember that on the night before he died for our sins, Jesus took bread, gave thanks for it, and shared the bread with his followers saying "Take eat, this is my body given for you. Do this in remembrance of me."

Likewise, he took the cup, gave thanks for it and passed it to his friends saying, "This cup is the new covenant in my blood. Do this as often as you drink it, in remembrance of me."

We remember, gracious God. We remember the covenant which you have made to us through Jesus Christ. We remember your call to us to be your church. We remember your commandment that we love and serve in your name.

This day we ask that your Holy Spirit descend upon these gifts of bread and cup. We ask that through them we might remember and recommit ourselves to you. We ask that through them we might know the presence of our risen Savior. This we ask, as your people.

Amen.

Times Of Difficulty

While written for congregational use, this prayer is also easily used for communion with shut-ins or people facing personal difficulties or illness.

The Lord be with you.
And also with you.
Lift up your hearts.
We lift them up to the Lord.
Let us give thanks to the Lord our God.
It is right to give God thanks and praise.

God of mercy, it is not always easy to give you thanks and praise. When our hearts ache and our spirits falter, it is difficult to think of anything other than ourselves and our pain.

In your mercy, remember us even when we forget about you.

God of love, you do not forsake us. When we wander, you seek us out. When we stumble, you support us. When we are in distress, you reach out to us.

In our time of need, surround us with your love and shelter us in your care.

God of grace, you provide for us. Through the words of scripture, through the compassion of others, through each new day, you offer us the possibility of life and the potential of a new tomorrow.

In our uncertainty, remind us of your presence and your promises.

God of hope, you know our need and answer it through your gifts to us. As we come before you with bread and cup, remind us again of what you have done for us through Jesus Christ and what you continue to do for us through your Holy Spirit.

For what is impossible for us is possible for you.

As we take this bread and break it, we remember Jesus' death upon the cross. As we share this bread, let your Spirit move among us and bring healing and peace.

For Jesus said, "This is my body which is broken for you."

As we take this cup and drink, we remember the new covenant made by Jesus. As we share this cup, let your Spirit fill us with assurance and comfort.

For Jesus said, "This is my blood which is poured out for the forgiveness of sins."

God of peace, let this time of communion be filled with more than simply the sharing of bread and cup. Let us taste the eternal and experience the possibilities that you have set before each of us. By your mercy, in your grace, and through your love, answer us in our time of need for we come before you God most holy, in Jesus' name.

Amen.

Celebration Of Women's Groups

The Lord be with you.
And also with you.
Lift up your hearts.
We lift them up to the Lord.
Let us give thanks to the Lord our God.
It is right to give God thanks and praise.

We do thank and praise you, loving God, for the good people who have shared their faith within the church and who have built up the body of Christ through their efforts. Throughout the ages, saints have walked among us teaching, preaching, and showing us what it means to be a disciple of Jesus Christ.

You have blessed us with women of vision in our congregation — dedicated women who served you in the women's groups of this church.

You have inspired and challenged us through these faithful servants. Through their fundraising we have been built up, by their dinners we have experienced fellowship, and in their prayers we have been supported and comforted.

As disciples, they encourage us in our walk of faith. As apostles, they call us to celebrate the gifts of God among us. As companions, they walk with us and support us by their service.

Gathered here this morning, we thank you for the women's groups that are part of our church. They have helped us be a strong and continual witness to the gospel of Jesus Christ in this place, across the country, and around the world.

They follow in faith and call us to follow in faith. They serve and invite us to serve. They remember Jesus Christ and help us to remember him.

On the night before he died, Jesus took bread, gave thanks for it, and shared it with his followers, asking them to remember him. He also took the cup, gave thanks for it, and shared it with his friends as a sign of the new promise God was making.

We remember and celebrate all that you have given us in Jesus Christ.

We pray for your Holy Spirit to descend upon us and upon these gifts of bread and cup. Allow us to see and hear and taste your goodness and promise. Allow us this food to strengthen our spirits and lives. Allow us to live and serve in Jesus' name.

Amen.

Seasons Of The Year

Summer

The Lord be with you.
And also with you.
Lift up your hearts.
We lift them up to the Lord.
Let us give thanks to the Lord our God.
It is right and good to give God thanks and praise.

God of the resurrection, we thank you for joy. In our world of darkness and gloom, you have shined the light of your love. The colors of the world, the creatures of the earth, and the majesty of the universe witness to the joy which is your work.

We praise you for Jesus, the joy of our hearts.

God of every new morning, we thank you for hope. In our world of uncertainty, you have brought us the promise of new beginnings. The words of scripture, the cycles of nature, the renewal of creation which goes on around us all testify to the hope which you have planted in all things.

We praise you for Jesus, our judge and our hope.

God of the law, we thank you for morality. In our world of conflicting values and opinions, you have laid out for us the right way to live. The law and the commandments, the example of good men and women, and the wisdom of those around us have shown us the better way.

We praise you for Jesus, who completes the law and the prophets.

God of the covenant, we thank you for faith. In our world of chaos and confusion, you have given us a foundation upon which to build. Through prayer, meditation, and service you cause us to draw closer to you and to each other.

We praise you for Jesus, through whom you make an everlasting promise of love.

God of all things seen and unseen, we thank you for spiritual gifts. In our world of isolation and fear, you have shown us the ties which bind us to you and each other. Through the caring smile, the kind word, the anonymous gift, you have blessed us and allowed us to be a blessing.

We thank you for Jesus, the way, the truth, and the life.

We remember that on the night before he died for our sins, Jesus broke the bread saying, "This is my body which is broken for you. Each time you eat this bread, remember me."

We remember the body of Jesus, broken on the cross.

We remember also that Jesus shared the cup saying, "This cup is the new covenant which God makes with you in my blood. Each time you drink from this cup, remember me."

We remember Jesus breaking the bonds of death, forever.

Send, we pray, your Holy Spirit upon these gifts of field and vine that through them we might taste the bread of life and the cup of salvation. For we ask this of you, heavenly Father, through Jesus Christ and in the unity of the Holy Spirit, one God forever and ever.

Amen.

Autumn

The Lord be with you.
And also with you.
Lift up your hearts.
We lift them up to the Lord.
Let us give thanks to the Lord our God.
It is right to give God thanks and praise.

We do thank and praise you, loving God, for the richness of the gifts you have given us. You have given us the bounty of creation, the bold colors of autumn, the cycles of nature, and the wonder of the earth around us. You have richly blessed us with a world of life and beauty.

You have given us women and men of vision to share our lives, prophets, saints, and teachers to lead us and teach us to follow you. You have given us people who tell of your goodness and show your love through their words and actions, and who touch our lives and the church with their service.

You have given us yourself in Jesus Christ. You came and dwelt among us as a tender infant, a youth, and an adult. You wept with those who wept and rejoiced with those who rejoiced. Through Jesus, you teach us about love and grace, mercy and service.

Through Jesus you invite us to be your people and call us to be faithful stewards of the gospel. For in the life of Jesus you have shown us such great self-giving love that even death upon a cross was not to be avoided.

You give us joy, eternal God. For on the third day you caused the resurrection to take place to shatter the sorrow of death. In its place you gave us the joy, hope, and promise of our risen Savior. For through Jesus you show us the way, the truth, and the life.

Gathered here this morning, we remember that on the night before he died, Jesus took bread, gave thanks for it, and shared it with his followers saying, "Take this, all of you, and eat it. This is my body, given for you. Each time you do this, remember me."

We remember that also that night, Jesus took the cup, gave thanks for it, and shared it with his friends saying, "This cup is the new covenant God has made with you in my blood. Each time you do this and drink from this cup, remember me." We remember, and we celebrate what you have given and continue to give to us in Jesus Christ.

Remembering Christ's death and celebrating his resurrection, we await with hope his coming again to bring peace and justice to the earth. For Christ has died, Christ is risen, and Christ will come again.

Gracious God, we pray for your Holy Spirit to descend upon us and upon these gifts of bread and cup. Allow us to see and hear and taste your goodness and the promise of eternal life. Fill us with strength, wisdom and renewed vigor to live as your people. This we ask in Jesus' name.

Amen.

Winter

The Lord be with you.
And also with you.
Lift up your hearts.
We lift them up to the Lord.
Let us give thanks to the Lord our God.
It is right and good to give God thanks and praise.

Eternal God, we thank you that in the quiet of the dark nights you are there. When the noise has hushed and the fevered pace of life has chilled, you draw us close and tell us that there is more than what we see.

"Be still and know that I am God."

When we cannot see an end to our troubles and are uncertain about what tomorrow will bring, you show us that change is possible. As the land rests under the blanket of snow and cold permeates the land and we worry, you remind us that there is a plan and a purpose.

"There is a time for everything under heaven."

In our distress you comfort us with peace and hope. As we look to the future with anxiety, you whisper about the possibility which is ours. When we dare to dream, you encourage us with glimpses of your vision and tastes of your promises.

"With Christ all things are possible."

Loving God, you lead us to the table that you have prepared for us. On the table you offer us bread to build up our strength and drink as a sign of your grace. You invite us to set aside everything that would stop us from seeing and knowing the beauty and joy around us. You offer us these gifts and invite us to be your people.

"We are more than conquerors through him who loved us."

As we take this bread and break it, we remember that on the night before Jesus died he took bread, broke it and offered it to his followers. He told them it was his body broken for them.

We remember Jesus' death upon the cross.

As we share this cup, we remember that on the night before he died Jesus took the cup and offered it to his followers. He told them it was his blood through which a new promise was being sealed.

We remember Jesus rising from the grave.

Gracious God, let your Holy Spirit move among us and transform these gifts and our lives. Allow us to see the eternal, experience the extraordinary, and be filled with your love once again. For we are your people and have come at your bidding in the name of Jesus Christ our Lord.

Amen.

Spring

The Lord be with you.
And also with you.
Lift up your hearts.
We lift them up to the Lord.
Let us give thanks to the Lord our God.
It is right to give God thanks and praise.

We give you thanks O God, for the majesty of the created world. With wonder we behold the changing seasons of the year, the splendor of new life in spring and the warmth of the long days of summer.

With awe we behold the beauty of autumn colors and the brightness of sunlit snow and ice in the cold of winter. As we look at the world, we marvel at all you have created for us.

We give you thanks, O God, for the diversity within nature. You crafted the rivers and oceans which continually move and flow and you shaped the mountains and hills which stand unchanging over the days but ever changing over the years.

You formed the meadows, forests, deserts, and tundras — each different in appearance and yet similar in their beauty and importance in creation. As we look at the world, we rejoice that you have provided all of us a place and a purpose within your kingdom.

We give you thanks, O God, for the interdependence of the created world. You have made all living things to interact and support each other. Every plant and animal connects in a cycle of life, death, and rebirth.

Each creature within creation has a place, and each season has a purpose. You have woven together all the elements of land, sea, and air to create life. As we look at the world, we are reminded that we are not alone but rather connected to you and to each other.

We give you thanks, O God, for you have called to us through Jesus Christ. You have called to us across lines of race, nationality, age, and experiences. You have invited each one of us to be your people and together to be your church.

You have given us gifts and skills to share with each other and with the world. You have given us opportunity and challenges to meet in faith. You have given us yourself in the person of Jesus Christ.

We thank you for Jesus Christ. For we remember that on the night before he died Jesus took bread, broke it, and said, "This is my body which is given for you. Each time you do this, remember me."

We remember that he also took the cup saying, "This cup is the new covenant God has made with you in my blood. Each time you do this and drink from this cup, remember me."

Send, we pray, your Holy Spirit, so that for us this bread might be the bread of life and for us this cup might be the cup of salvation. Allow your Spirit to bless these gifts that we might be refreshed and inspired in our faith and service as we share together these signs of your love, through Jesus Christ.

Amen.

Life Of Jesus

Life Of Jesus (1)

The Lord be with you.
And also with you.
Lift up your hearts.
We lift them up to the Lord.
Let us give thanks to the Lord our God.
It is right to give God thanks and praise.

We give you thanks and praise, O God, that you created humanity to live in the world and know you. You gave us the prophets to teach us your will and the law to guide us. Through the law and the prophets, you gave us your promise of a Messiah who would lead us to salvation.

We give you thanks that in the fullness of time you completed the law and the prophets, through your only Son, Jesus:

Jesus, the baby born at Bethlehem, tiny and helpless;

Jesus, raised by Mary and Joseph, the boy who grew in wisdom and stature and found favor in your eyes;

Jesus, the adult, who faced temptation in the desert;

Jesus, the teacher, who showed your mercy and love.

Through Jesus, humble before heaven and obedient unto death, you have shown us what it means to be human.

We give you thanks that through Jesus you have shown us more than mere humanity, for you came and dwelt among us as Jesus:

Jesus Christ, who was anointed by the Holy Spirit at his baptism;

Jesus Christ, who shone on the mountaintop with divine radiance;

Jesus Christ, blameless and without sin, who was killed upon a cross;

Jesus Christ, who burst the bonds of death and sin and lives forevermore;

Jesus Christ, who ascended into heaven and who sits at God's right hand.

Through Jesus, you show us the true extent of your unstoppable forgiveness, grace, and love.

We thank you this day and every day for Jesus Christ. Through Jesus, you call us to be your people. Through Jesus, you have shown us the way, the truth, and the life. Through Jesus, you make a new and eternal covenant with us.

On the night before Jesus died, he took bread, broke it, and said, "This is my body which is given for you. Each time you do this, remember me." He also took the cup saying, "This cup is the new covenant God has made with you in my blood. Each time you do this and drink from this cup, remember me."

Send, we pray, your Holy Spirit upon these gifts of bread and cup that for us they might become for us the body and blood of our Lord that we might share in his life and in his way. We ask this in the name of Jesus Christ our Savior and Lord.

Amen.

Life Of Jesus (2)

The Lord be with you.
And also with you.
Lift up your hearts.
We lift them up to the Lord.
Let us give God thanks and praise.
It is right to give God thanks and praise.

We give you thanks, holy God, for the teaching and witness of Jesus Christ. The record of scripture reveals to us the parables and wisdom he taught all disciples. The testimony of those who followed him bears witness to his life, death, and resurrection.

Help us to carry his words with us so that we might be a people informed and excited by the gospel message.

We give you thanks, eternal God, for the life, death, and resurrection of Jesus Christ. The suffering and trials of Jesus, as well as the despair of the cross, show your great love for us. The triumph of the empty tomb and the presence of our risen Lord reveal the mystery and wonder of your grace.

Help us to embody your living Word that we might live as bold people of faith.

We thank you for this table and the gifts upon it. We thank you for the bread of life and the body broken upon the cross for our sins. We thank you for the cup of our salvation and the blood shed to seal the new covenant.

Help us to experience the great love and sacrifice which makes this meal communion with you.

As we come before this table, we remember that Jesus broke the bread saying, "This is my body which is broken for you. Do this in remembrance of me."

We break this bread. We eat and remember.

As we come to this table, we remember that Jesus shared the cup saying, "This cup is the new covenant in my blood. Do this, as often as you drink it, in remembrance of me."

We share the cup. We drink and remember.

Send, we pray, your Holy Spirit upon this table, that as we feast upon these gifts they might be for us the body and blood of our Lord Jesus Christ.

Allow us to draw near to you and share this bread and cup as a sign of our faith and trust in the power of your love and grace.

This we ask, holy and eternal God, in the name of Jesus and in the unity of the Holy Spirit, one God, forever and ever.

Amen.

Life Of Jesus (3)

The Lord be with you.
And also with you.
Lift up your hearts.
We lift them up to the Lord.
Let us give God thanks and praise.
It is right and good to give God thanks and praise.

We thank and praise you, eternal God, for you have sent your son Jesus Christ into the world to reclaim us. Your answer to our world lost in sin was a Savior with the power to set us free and return us to your kingdom.

Jesus said, "I am the way, and the truth, and the life."

We thank and praise you, loving God, for Jesus Christ who has shown us your face and has spoken your words to a weary world. Jesus in his life showed us your way and allowed us to hope of life eternal with you.

Jesus said, "Whoever has seen me has seen my Father."

We thank and praise you, merciful God, for Jesus Christ who emptied himself and became a servant to all. He took upon himself our sins and suffered for our sakes. He was wounded for our transgressions and was killed to break the power of sin and death.

Jesus said, "This is my body, which is broken for you."

Take this bread and bless it, we pray, that it might be for us the body of Christ.

Jesus said, "This is my blood which is shed for you."

Take this cup and bless it, we pray, that it might be for us the blood of Christ.

Jesus said on the cross, "It is finished."

Renew us as we share this bread and cup. Renew our weary spirits, fill our hearts with your love, and open our eyes to see the meaning and purpose of Christ's death upon the cross and his rising from the grave. Hear our prayer, God most holy, in the name of Jesus, the Lamb of heaven, in the unity of the Holy Spirit, one God, forever and ever.

Amen.

Prayers After Communion

Prayers After Communion

We thank you, gracious God,
that you have refreshed us at your table.
Allow us to go forth from this place as your people,
filled with the Holy Spirit, speaking your good news,
and serving in Christ's name.
Amen.

* * *

We thank and praise you, eternal God,
that you have refreshed us at your table through your Holy Spirit.
Fill us with hope, and peace, and zeal,
that we might live and serve in Jesus' name.
Amen.

* * *

Gracious God, for the bread of life and for the cup of salvation,
we thank you. Allow us to go forth from this table
and live as your holy people,
rejoicing in the power of your Holy Spirit
and walking in the way of Jesus Christ.
Amen.

* * *

Lord Jesus, bread of life and the true vine,
we have remembered your death upon the cross
and the new covenant made in your blood.
Fill us now with the zeal and passion to go out in the world
and bear witness to your love.
Amen.

* * *

Eternal and gracious God,
we have tasted your goodness yet again this day.
Send us forth filled with the Holy Spirit
to live and serve as people of the resurrection.
Allow us to be both witnesses and agents of your grace,
through Jesus Christ our Lord.
Amen.

* * *

Heavenly Father, we have eaten the bread of life
and drunk from the cup of salvation.
Send us forth now to be your people,
living, serving, and loving, in Jesus' way.
Amen.

* * *

Eternal and loving God, for the bread which we have eaten
and the cup we have tasted, we praise and thank you.
For you have touched us by your Holy Spirit,
and challenged us to live as your people,
through Jesus Christ our Lord.
Amen.

www.ingramcontent.com/pod-product-compliance
Lightning Source LLC
LaVergne TN
LVHW020652100826
845148LV00012B/2448

* 9 7 8 0 7 8 8 0 2 4 8 7 0 *